Original title:
Affection's Architecture

Copyright © 2024 Swan Charm
All rights reserved.

Author: Swan Charm
ISBN HARDBACK: 978-9916-86-683-2
ISBN PAPERBACK: 978-9916-86-684-9
ISBN EBOOK: 978-9916-86-685-6

The Layout of Togetherness

In whispers shared beneath the stars,
We sketch our dreams with gentle scars.
The canvas holds our laughter bright,
A tapestry of heart and light.

Each moment layered, side by side,
In every sigh, our hopes abide.
The colors blend, a vibrant hue,
Creating worlds where love feels new.

Through storms we walk, hand in hand,
In unity, we make our stand.
The path may twist, but we'll be strong,
With voices soft, we'll sing our song.

A quilt of memories, stitched with care,
In every fabric, warmth we share.
Together woven, with threads so fine,
In the layout of our hearts, you're mine.

So here's to the moments we create,
In every heartbeat, love won't wait.
Together, forever, our spirits soar,
In the layout of togetherness, we explore.

Bridges of Gentle Words

Whispers flow like soft streams,
Connecting hearts with tender beams.
In every syllable, a bridge is laid,
Uniting souls, where love is made.

Echoes linger in the night,
Every word a guiding light.
Through laughter, tears, and silent grace,
We build a world, a warm embrace.

Crafting Skies of Affection

With gentle hands, we shape the air,
Colors blend, a canvas rare.
Each stroke a story yet untold,
In skies of love, our dreams unfold.

Clouds of hope drift soft and wide,
As hearts entwine, side by side.
In every hue, a promise shines,
A tapestry where love aligns.

Foundation Stones of Memory

Each moment adds to what we build,
With laughter, tears, our hearts are filled.
Stone by stone, the past we lay,
A fortress strong, come what may.

Echoes of joy, whispers of pain,
We gather close in sun and rain.
In every brick, our stories gleam,
A sacred bond, a timeless dream.

The Fabric of Silent Affection

In quiet threads, our love is sewn,
A tapestry that feels like home.
Every glance, a stitch so fine,
In woven hearts, our spirits shine.

The colors blend, so soft, so bright,
In silence, we share the light.
Through every fold, emotions flow,
A fabric rich, with hearts that glow.

Portals to Promise

In the hush of twilight's glow,
Whispers of dreams begin to flow.
Through the gateway of the night,
Hopeful stars shine ever bright.

Every path has tales to tell,
Voices soft as a wishing well.
Step inside, embrace the call,
In this realm, we rise, we fall.

Colors blend, a vibrant sight,
Painting futures, pure delight.
With every heartbeat, we explore,
Portals open, hearts can soar.

Unseen threads weave our fates,
Kaleidoscopes of love that waits.
In the silence, bonds ignite,
Radiant dreams take their flight.

Together, we unlock the door,
To tomorrow and so much more.
Hand in hand, we journey forth,
Building bridges of great worth.

Blueprints of the Heart

Within the lines our stories lie,
Blueprints drawn beneath the sky.
Each emotion, a gentle trace,
Mapping love in every space.

Dreams constructed, firm and true,
Brick by brick, we'll see it through.
In this framework, we will grow,
Ties that bind, the love we sow.

The architect of fleeting time,
Designing moments, pure and prime.
Every glance, a measured part,
Crafting lives with a hopeful heart.

When shadows fall, we find the light,
Guided by a shared insight.
Lines may bend, yet never break,
Always stronger for our sake.

Let's forge a path, a sacred space,
Where dreams and love will interlace.
With plans in hand, we chart the way,
Foundations strong for every day.

Foundations of Warmth

In the glow of a crackling fire,
Warmth spreads deep, igniting desire.
Gathered close, we share our tales,
Each laugh and sigh, the heart prevails.

Blankets wrapped, we find our peace,
In simple moments, joys increase.
The world outside fades away,
Nestled here, we choose to stay.

With cups of tea, we toast to life,
Amidst the chaos, free from strife.
Connections made with every breath,
Embracing all, defying death.

Seasons change, yet hearts remain,
Through every trial, love sustains.
Foundations built on trust and care,
A sanctuary, always there.

So let us gather, night or day,
In warmth and laughter, find our way.
Together, we create our spark,
A legacy to light the dark.

Arched Windows of Whimsy

Through the arches, colors play,
Sunlight dances, bright as day.
Whispers of dreams in the air,
Magic lingers, everywhere.

Clouds like cotton, drifting slow,
Hopeful hearts begin to glow.
Each window frames a world anew,
Where laughter sparkles like the dew.

Glimmers of joy in every hue,
Stories waiting, just for you.
Imagination takes its flight,
Painting memories in the light.

Breezes carry secrets near,
Softly spoken, sweet and clear.
Every glance a gentle trace,
In this place, we find our space.

With each arch, a tale unfolds,
Wonders whispered, dreams retold.
Together in this vibrant song,
In these windows, we belong.

The Sanctuary of Shared Laughter

In the sanctuary, joy resides,
Laughter echoes, love abides.
A circle formed, our hearts unwind,
In the warmth, our souls aligned.

Stories shared with every smile,
Time slows down, just for a while.
The world outside fades away,
Here in laughter's bright array.

Every voice a melody sweet,
With each chuckle, our hearts meet.
Together we weave this delight,
In shared laughter, hearts take flight.

Moments cherished, bonds that grow,
In this haven, we all glow.
Joyful spirits, hand in hand,
Creating memories, oh so grand.

As the sun sets, shadows play,
But our laughter lights the way.
In this space, we've found our place,
Together, forever, in grace.

Carved Dreams into Tomorrow

Carved in whispers, dreams take form,
Shaped by hopes, they keep us warm.
Each vision glimmers, strong and bright,
Guiding us through darkest night.

With chiseled faith, we shape our fate,
Planting seeds, we celebrate.
In the garden of our desire,
We watch our dreams ignite and inspire.

Tomorrow holds a canvas wide,
Each stroke reveals a heartfelt guide.
Together we craft our design,
In every heartbeat, spirits shine.

As we etch our paths ahead,
On the tapestry, dreams are spread.
With open hearts, we rise and soar,
Carving legacies, evermore.

In the kaleidoscope of life,
We navigate through joy and strife.
Hand in hand, let's pave the way,
For dreams that live, come what may.

Haven of Mutual Growth

In a haven where kindness thrives,
Connections grow, the spirit strives.
Roots entwined, we share the sun,
Together we flourish, everyone.

With open hearts, we nurture care,
As dreams take flight in warm, fresh air.
Supporting each other, side by side,
In this refuge, our hopes abide.

Every challenge becomes a chance,
To learn, to leap, to take a stance.
Unified, our visions glow,
In this garden, love will flow.

With patience, we cultivate the soil,
Through storms and trials, we will toil.
Yet in the rain, we find our cheer,
In this haven, we persevere.

As seasons change and time proceeds,
We harvest joy from planted seeds.
In a world where we both thrive,
Together, we feel so alive.

Blueprints of the Heart

In shadows soft, dreams weave tight,
A canvas drawn in fading light.
Each line a wish, each curve a plea,
Blueprints hidden, longing to be free.

With whispers low, hopes start to bloom,
Scattered sketches fill the room.
A work of art, yet to unfold,
In every heart, a story told.

From depths of love, we find our way,
A path through night, towards the day.
With ink and grace, we seek to chart,
The endless love that fills the heart.

The Framework of Embrace

From gentle hands, a shelter grows,
Where warmth surrounds and kindness flows.
Each touch a frame, a tender hold,
In bonds of love, our stories told.

Through whispered dreams, we build and bind,
A place where souls in peace can find.
With every laugh, and every tear,
The structure stands, steadfast and clear.

In fleeting moments, our hearts entwine,
Finding solace, in love's design.
Together strong, we rise above,
Constructing life, with threads of love.

Foundations of Tenderness

In quiet corners, hearts will rest,
Upon the ground where love's addressed.
Each beat a stone, so firm and true,
Foundations laid, for me and you.

With every trust, we deepen roots,
In soil of grace, where kindness shoots.
Compassion's rain will gently fall,
A bounteous gift, for one and all.

In tender words, we carve our space,
Creating havens, filled with grace.
In the depths of care, we find our way,
A sanctuary, where hearts can stay.

Pillars of Warmth

Amidst the storms, our love remains,
Pillars strong, through joy and pains.
With open arms, we stand so tall,
Embracing each, we never fall.

Through seasons change, we hold the ground,
In echoes sweet, our hearts resound.
A lighthouse bright upon the shore,
Guiding dreams forevermore.

In every glance, in every sigh,
Warmth of our bond will never die.
Together forged, through fire and rain,
Our pillars stand, despite the strain.

Castles of Comfort

In the warm glow of the hearth,
We gather to share our dreams,
The walls hum with laughter's mirth,
In the shadows, love redeems.

Each room cloaked in gentle light,
Soft whispers dance on the breeze,
Outside, the world fades to night,
Inside, we find our hearts at ease.

The kitchen fills with fragrant meals,
Memories rise with the steam,
Our joy is a treasure that heals,
In this space, we reign supreme.

Windows frame the starry skies,
Guardians of our sacred time,
Through them, every wish also flies,
Each moment feels like a rhyme.

A castle built not with stone,
But with warmth, laughter, and cheer,
These walls hold a love that's grown,
In our hearts, forever near.

Anchored Hearts

In the tempest, we are bound,
Holding fast through stormy winds,
Our love like roots in the ground,
Together, each challenge rescinds.

Words unsaid feel like the tide,
Pulling closer, drifting apart,
In your gaze, I confide,
You have always known my heart.

Through the waves, our spirits soar,
Casting nets into the deep,
In your presence, I explore,
The promises that we keep.

When shadows threaten the day,
You are my harbor, my light,
In your arms, I drift and sway,
A safe haven through the night.

Anchors set in trust and care,
Two souls entwined, forever sworn,
With each heartbeat, we declare,
A love that can never be worn.

Sturdy Threads of Connection

In the fabric of our days,
Interwoven, forms a bond,
Through laughter and through praise,
A tapestry that goes beyond.

Every thread, a story spun,
Colors bright and dark unite,
In the warmth of the rising sun,
We find strength in shared delight.

With gentle hands, we craft our lives,
Stitching moments, both big and small,
In this union, we both thrive,
Together, we rise, never fall.

The loom of time weaves us tight,
Patterns shifting, yet so clear,
In the softness of the night,
Love's design draws us near.

As seasons change with each new pass,
We hold fast to what we know,
Sturdy threads that will not trespass,
Through every trial, we will grow.

Rooms of Reflection

In quiet corners, thoughts collide,
Mirrored walls show who we are,
In solitude, we gently bide,
Finding peace beneath the stars.

Each room beckons with its grace,
Soft lighting, a serene embrace,
Memories linger in this space,
A sanctuary, a sacred place.

Windows framed with gentle light,
Inviting dreams to find their way,
Silent echoes in the night,
Whisper secrets we can say.

Worn-out books on dusty shelves,
Pages turning, histories told,
Here we discover ourselves,
In the past, our hearts grow bold.

Rooms that cradle every thought,
In their silence, wisdom grows,
Lessons learned and battles fought,
In reflection, love still flows.

Rhythm of Resonance

In the hush of night we sway,
Echoes dance, gently play.
Hearts beat as one, a shared song,
In this moment, we belong.

Stars above begin to glow,
Filling silence, soft and slow.
Each note bends with the breeze,
Carried far through the trees.

Whispers linger, sweet and clear,
Melodies that draw us near.
Time stops, as the world fades,
In this rhythm, love cascades.

A symphony of shared dreams,
Flowing gently, like the streams.
Hands entwined, we start to glide,
In the music, there's no pride.

Let this dance forever last,
Forget the worries of the past.
Together we are meant to find,
A resonance that's truly blind.

Craftsmanship of Care

Hands that shape with tender grace,
Every curve, a warm embrace.
Building trust with every thread,
In this craft, our love is bred.

Through the hours, patience finds,
Artistry that gently binds.
Chiseling out each intricate part,
Molding strength within the heart.

So we carve our lives with flair,
Detailed paths that we both share.
Every stroke, a choice we make,
In this creation, souls awake.

Time unfolds with every chance,
A masterpiece in every glance.
Together working, hand in hand,
In this space, we understand.

For it's love that shapes the clay,
In this beauty, we will stay.
Craftsmanship of care declared,
Through our bond, we are repaired.

The Layout of Love

In the garden, paths entwine,
Blossoms bloom, a grand design.
Each petal whispers, soft and true,
Mapping out the dreams for two.

Sunlight filters through the trees,
Gently swaying with the breeze.
Each turn leads where hearts align,
In the layout, love's divine.

Steps we take upon this ground,
Echo forth with joy unbound.
Every corner, every trace,
Crafted with a warm embrace.

Seasons change, but we remain,
Through the joy and through the pain.
Hand in hand, we guide the way,
In this layout, here we'll stay.

With every path that we design,
We weave our stories, intertwine.
In the layout built by trust,
Together bloom, for love is a must.

Spires of Connection

Reaching high, we touch the sky,
Spires of dreams that never die.
Built on hope, and love combined,
In this journey, we're aligned.

Through the clouds, we brave the storms,
In connection, our heart warms.
Foundations strong beneath our feet,
In the climb, we find our beat.

Every twilight, stars appear,
Lighting up the path we steer.
As we rise, there's strength in grace,
In the spires, we find our place.

Voices merge in harmony,
Creating bonds that set us free.
Each moment shared, we rise above,
In these spires, we find our love.

Together we will reach the peak,
In this silence, hearts will speak.
Spires of connection, tall and proud,
In our unity, we're avowed.

The Structure of Embrace

In the warmth of silence, we find,
The gentle pull of hands entwined.
Each moment whispers, soft and clear,
Creating bonds that hold us near.

Walls of trust, unyielding stand,
Crafted by love, an intimate hand.
Through storms and sun, our roots grow deep,
In this embrace, our hearts will keep.

Each beam of laughter, bright and bold,
A treasure trove of stories told.
Together we rise, we ebb and flow,
In the structure of embrace, love will grow.

Through shadows cast and daylight bright,
We build our dreams, ignite the night.
Each touch a promise, every glance,
A dance of souls in timeless trance.

Here in this space, we find our place,
A sanctuary, a tender grace.
Embraced by time, we'll never part,
Together, forever, heart to heart.

Designed by Devotion

With every thread of golden hue,
A tapestry of me and you.
Stitched by hope, wove in dreams,
Together, we create our themes.

Blueprints drawn with love's own hand,
Plans that no heart could withstand.
Each moment crafted with intent,
A masterpiece, no time to spend.

In the quiet hours, we align,
Two souls entwined, your heart in mine.
Built on promises, strong and true,
In every plan, it's me and you.

Windows open, letting light,
Into our world, so pure and bright.
Designed by devotion, bold and free,
A home where love is meant to be.

In every laugh, in every tear,
The strength of us grows year by year.
A structure vast and deeply sown,
In love's embrace, we are at home.

Pillars of Togetherness

Standing tall, our pillars rise,
Holding dreams beneath the skies.
Each one built on faith and trust,
A legacy of love, a must.

Branches intertwine, roots deep,
In this bond, our hearts we keep.
Together we weather all life's storms,
In every shape, our love transforms.

With whispered joys and stories shared,
We're building arches, love declared.
Each laughter rings like chimes that play,
Strengthening us, come what may.

In the shadows and in the light,
We forge our path, hearts taking flight.
Pillars strong, supporting each day,
In togetherness, we find our way.

Through every chapter, thick and thin,
Our journey starts and then begins.
Erected high, each pillar stands,
A testament of our joined hands.

The Framework of Love

An outline drawn with tender lines,
A vision where our heart defines.
In every angle, every curve,
The framework stands, we find our nerve.

With laughter echoing in the halls,
We build a space where love enthralls.
Each beam holds stories yet untold,
The warmth of us, a joy to hold.

From the foundation, strong and wide,
We rise together, side by side.
Crafted in moments, day by day,
The framework of love lights our way.

Windows open to the stars,
Inviting dreams, erasing scars.
In this embrace, we feel so free,
A perfect fit, just you and me.

Together we frame our brightest days,
In love's design, we find our ways.
Each heartbeat echoes, soft and sweet,
In the framework of love, we are complete.

Scaffolding Souls

In the twilight of our dreams,
We build a space for love's beams.
Each gentle thought a sturdy plank,
Each whispered word an open tank.

Together we rise, side by side,
A structure strong, where hearts confide.
Through storms we brace, in sun we thrive,
In this embrace, our souls arrive.

With every laugh, a layer laid,
With every tear, foundations made.
In harmony, we craft and mold,
A refuge warm against the cold.

As beams of trust intertwine,
Our spirits dance, they leap, they shine.
Brick by brick, we claim our place,
In this grand blueprint full of grace.

So here we stand, in our high tower,
Two souls together, a blooming flower.
In scaffolding, we find our whole,
Bound forever, we scaffold souls.

The Harmony of Hearts

In every note, a love we share,
A melody that fills the air.
With beats that dance in perfect time,
Our hearts compose a sweet, soft rhyme.

Each chord we strike, a sign of trust,
In harmony, our souls combust.
Together we sing, with voices blend,
In symphony until the end.

A rhythm builds, a gentle sway,
In this embrace, we find our way.
With every breath, a promise made,
In songs of love, we won't evade.

Our spirits soar, like birds in flight,
Creating day from endless night.
The harmony of hearts resounds,
In love's pure light, our truth abounds.

So let the music play and flow,
In this sweet dance, we always grow.
With every heartbeat, we will start,
An endless song, the harmony of hearts.

Framing Our Feelings

With every brush, emotions flow,
In vibrant hues, our passions show.
We paint the canvas, bold and bright,
Framing feelings in the light.

Each stroke a story, every shade,
Of laughter shared and tears displayed.
In colors rich, our lives align,
A masterpiece that's truly mine.

Our hearts the frames that gently hold,
The art of truths both shy and bold.
In every corner, warmth we find,
In the gallery of heart and mind.

With patience thick, the layers dry,
As time unveils the reasons why.
In this creation, we define,
Our love's deep roots, forever twine.

So let us craft, with tender hands,
A life where each emotion stands.
As time ticks on, we will reveal,
The beauty found in framing feelings.

The Interlace of Trust

In gentle threads, our lives entwine,
A tapestry of yours and mine.
With every stitch, the bonds we weave,
In quiet moments, we believe.

Through trials faced, our fibers blend,
In strength we find, we never bend.
A pattern rich in hues that shine,
In this embrace, our hearts align.

Each knot a promise, tightly bound,
In whispers soft, our truths are found.
With hands held fast, we face the night,
The interlace that feels so right.

Through shadows cast, we find our way,
In trust's embrace, we shall not sway.
In knots of love, we find our strength,
Together we can go the lengths.

So here we stand, united whole,
In woven paths, we share our soul.
Together, always, we can trust,
In the interlace of love, we must.

Pathways of Passion

In twilight's glow, we walk as one,
Hearts beat loud, our journey begun.
Through silent woods and rivers wide,
In love's embrace, we take our stride.

The stars above light our way,
Guiding dreams that softly sway.
With every step, we leave a trace,
In the garden of time, we find our place.

The winds whisper secrets down the lane,
Of laughter shared and patches of rain.
Together we rise, we bend, we grow,
On pathways of passion, forever we flow.

Each sunrise paints a vibrant scene,
Where hopes ignite and worries glean.
In moments captured, we take a chance,
Through every tear, we learn to dance.

With hands entwined and eyes aglow,
We face the world with hearts in tow.
In the tapestry of life, our hues blend,
Pathways of passion, with love to transcend.

Weaving Whispers

In the quiet of night, whispers roam,
Soft secrets shared, the heart feels home.
Threads of silence, gentle and light,
Weaving dreams in the tapestry of night.

Through fluttering leaves, a story we weave,
With every sigh, we learn to believe.
Tales of wonder, both near and far,
In the fabric of time, we find who we are.

Delicate voices float on the breeze,
Bridging the gaps, bringing us ease.
In moments fleeting, we find our grace,
Weaving whispers, a sacred space.

With moonlit paths, we tread so slow,
Hand in hand, we let our truths flow.
In every shadow, our laughter sings,
Weaving whispers, the joy it brings.

So let us gather each soft-spoken word,
In the melody of love, let's be heard.
In this world of silence, we'll take our chance,
With weaving whispers, our hearts will dance.

The Tapestry of Together

Fingers entwined, we craft our fate,
In the loom of life, we create our state.
Colorful threads in shades of bright,
The tapestry of together ignites the night.

Stitched with laughter, sewn with care,
In every pattern, a memory shared.
Moments of joy and tears unite,
In the art of love, we take flight.

With every heartbeat, a thread intertwined,
Stories of us like stars aligned.
In the gentle glow of the evening sky,
The tapestry of together will never die.

Embroidered dreams and hopes so high,
In the fabric of time, we learn to fly.
With strength and grace, we'll face the storm,
Together we rise, in each other, we're warm.

In this vast world, our colors blend,
A beautiful journey that knows no end.
In the weave of our lives, love will forever stay,
The tapestry of together, guiding our way.

Solid Bonds and Gentle Spaces

In moments shared, we build the trust,
Solid bonds formed, in love we must.
With every laugh, with every tear,
We create a haven, so warm and near.

Through trials faced and battles fought,
Gentle spaces are the lessons taught.
In whispered voices, we find our way,
Solid bonds that forever stay.

With open hearts and minds we share,
In the dance of life, we show we care.
Through shifting tides, we find our place,
Solid bonds and gentle spaces.

With every heartbeat, we make a vow,
To cherish the moments, here and now.
In the embrace of love, we see,
Solid bonds and gentle spaces, we'll always be.

So here we stand, side by side,
In the journey of life, our hearts collide.
Together we grow, in sun and in rain,
Solid bonds and gentle spaces, forever remain.

Love's Structural Secrets

In shadows where the whispers meet,
A heartbeat echoes, soft and sweet.
Two souls entwined, a silent pact,
In every glance, the truth intact.

The arches of passion, strong yet thin,
Foundations built from where we begin.
With every laugh, the walls draw near,
Crafting solace, erasing fear.

The beams of trust hold weight and grace,
Together we have carved this space.
In love's design, we sketch our fate,
With every moment, we celebrate.

A symphony of hands in motion,
Tendrils of care, a deep devotion.
Our blueprint sketched beneath the stars,
In every hug, love's secret bars.

With every heartbeat, we align,
A structure built, a sacred sign.
In love's embrace, we find the key,
As hidden walls set our hearts free.

The Design of Intimacy

In quiet corners where we dwell,
Whispers bloom like secrets to tell.
Every touch a thread finely spun,
Creating warmth, two hearts as one.

Lines drawn softly in gentle space,
The comfort found in close embrace.
A map unfolded, paths intertwined,
In the depths of love, we redefine.

The windows open to dreams anew,
Breezes of hope, just me and you.
In this canvas, brush strokes blend,
Artistry of hearts, we intend.

Bound by laughter, we lay our schemes,
Found in the quiet of shared dreams.
With every heartbeat, our story grows,
An intricate dance, in love it flows.

As shadows deepen, we find the way,
Through every dawn, through night and day.
In this design, our lives align,
In the structure of love, we brightly shine.

Crafting Connections

Threads of golden warmth we weave,
In the fabric of trust, we believe.
With every word, a stitch is made,
Building bridges that will not fade.

Hands held tightly, guiding the way,
In the light of love, we brightly stay.
Every shared laugh, a colored thread,
In the tapestry of life we tread.

A gentle touch, a soothing balm,
In this union, we find our calm.
Crafting memories, each one bright,
In the gallery of shared delight.

Layer by layer, our hearts unfold,
The warmth of connection, a story told.
In this creation, we do not fear,
The bond of love pulls us near.

As seasons change and days transform,
In the storm of life, we stay warm.
Crafting a future with open hands,
Together we stand, as fate commands.

Walls Built with Kindness

Bricks of care laid one by one,
In the glow of kindness, we are done.
With every smile, a wall grows tall,
A fortress strong where love won't fall.

Painted hues of laughter bright,
In the gentle glow of soft moonlight.
Every word a sturdy stone,
Creating spaces we call home.

The roof of dreams shields us from strife,
In this shelter, we share our life.
With open doors and hearts like skies,
Together, we will rise and rise.

The windows sparkle with hope's embrace,
In the warmth of kindness, we find our place.
Bound by love, we break the mold,
In this haven, our story is told.

As seasons pass, our walls will stand,
Crafted with care by patient hands.
In the heart of kindness, we will thrive,
These walls of love will keep us alive.

The Framework of Forever

In shadows cast by dreams we weave,
A canvas bright with hopes conceived.
Each moment frames the life we share,
Together built, beyond compare.

The stars align in tranquil skies,
With whispered truths and gentle sighs.
Our hearts compose a timeless song,
In harmony, we both belong.

Through storms that test our will and might,
We find our paths, forever bright.
In every challenge, love prevails,
Our bond, an echo that never fails.

With every dawn, a chance to grow,
In spaces where our feelings flow.
The framework strong, it holds us tight,
Constructed from both day and night.

So let us dance through endless time,
As rhythms blend, our hearts will climb.
In layers rich, our story spun,
The framework of forever won.

Cemented Connections

In twilight's glow, our whispers meet,
A bond unbroken, strong and sweet.
With every laugh, a brick we lay,
In cemented love, we find our way.

Through trials deep and valleys low,
Our roots entwine, together grow.
Each memory forged, a sturdy wall,
In every rise, we shall not fall.

In quiet moments, strength we find,
A steadfast heart, forever kind.
The mortar warms, through cold and heat,
A universe in every heartbeat.

With each new day, our dreams expand,
As we design our future planned.
Bound not by walls but endless skies,
Cemented connections, you and I.

So hand in hand, we'll pave the street,
Together brave, we face the heat.
For in this life, one truth prevails,
Through love's embrace, we set our sails.

The Tapestry of Togetherness

Threads of life, in colors bright,
We weave a world, our shared delight.
Each moment stitches, memories flow,
The tapestry of us will grow.

In laughter and tears, we find the hue,
A masterpiece crafted, me and you.
Patterns emerge from time well spent,
In every touch, love's intent.

With shadows that dance in the evening light,
We hold each other through the night.
Bold strokes of passion and gentle grace,
Together forever, we find our place.

In every stitch, a story told,
Of bonds unyielding and hearts of gold.
Entwined we stand, against the fray,
The tapestry of us, here to stay.

So weave with me, in dreams so wide,
As we create, side by side.
For in this life, our colors blend,
Tapestry of togetherness, without end.

Foundations Beneath Our Feet

In quiet strength, our roots entwine,
A bedrock firm, where hopes align.
Through shifting sands, we find our ground,
Foundations strong, forever sound.

With every storm that tests our will,
We stand as one, through good and ill.
The earth beneath, our solemn vow,
With passions deep, we flourish now.

In whispered dreams, our voices rise,
Untouched by fear, we claim the skies.
Each step we take, a stone we lay,
Foundations beneath us day by day.

With open hearts and arms outstretched,
We build a world we both have etched.
Through years that pass, our love's decree,
A haven found, just you and me.

So let us walk, these paths we tread,
With every breath, a life well-fed.
For in this place, our roots run deep,
Foundations strong, in love we seep.

Arches of Understanding

In the shadows, hearts align,
Beneath the arches, spirits twine.
Words like rivers freely flow,
In silence, deeper truths we know.

With open minds, we bridge the gap,
In knowing looks, no need for maps.
The paths we've walked, the stories shared,
In every gaze, a warmth declared.

In laughter's echo, we find grace,
Each moment shared, a sacred space.
We build our trust with gentle hands,
In understanding, love expands.

Through trials faced, our bond grows strong,
In every note, we sing along.
Together we rise, hand in hand,
On arches built, forever stand.

So let us cherish, let us thrive,
In every heart, our truth alive.
For arches of understanding hold,
A universe of dreams untold.

Constructions of Kindness

With bricks of hope, we lay the ground,
A fortress built where love is found.
In every gesture, kindness grows,
A warm embrace, the heart bestows.

Through every act, a spark ignites,
In simple deeds, the world ignites.
From whispered words to helping hands,
Compassion builds, the spirit stands.

In shadows cast, a light we find,
Together we weave, heart aligned.
With every smile, we share the load,
In kindness, we lighten the road.

Through storms we face, we stand as one,
In unity, we can't be undone.
Each brick we lay, a story spun,
In constructions of kindness, we have won.

So let our hearts, like hammers strike,
To build a world where love feels right.
In kindness, we find our way,
Creating light in every day.

The Canvas of Companionship

On the canvas, colors blend,
Each stroke, a story, hearts extend.
With laughter bright and whispers low,
In every hue, our friendship grows.

From dawn to dusk, we paint the day,
In shared moments, we find our way.
Through trials faced, we mix our tones,
From vibrant greens to softened stones.

In every tear, a palette blooms,
Together we fill the empty rooms.
With brushes dipped in dreams we share,
The canvas lives with love and care.

Through every shade, our spirits rise,
In this gallery, no goodbyes.
In strokes of gold, our futures blend,
On this canvas, hearts transcend.

A masterpiece of trust we weave,
In every moment, we believe.
For in companionship, we find our place,
A work of art, our hearts embrace.

Harmony in Every Corner

In whispers soft, the echoes play,
A song of peace, we find each day.
In every corner, kindness sings,
In unity, the heart takes wings.

With open hearts, we share the space,
In harmony, we find our grace.
Through trials thick, our voices blend,
In every struggle, love will mend.

With every smile, the world ignites,
In shared moments, joy takes flight.
From darkest nights to mornings bright,
In harmony, we chase the light.

Together we rise, a chorus bold,
In every story, warmth retold.
Through laughter and tears, we stand as one,
In harmony, our hearts have won.

So let us cherish every sound,
In every corner, joy is found.
For life's a song, with notes we share,
In harmony, we breathe the air.

Building the Bonds of Care

In tender moments shared, we grow,
Each smile a seed, each touch a glow.
With every heartbeat, trust awakes,
Together we stand, for love's own sake.

Through laughter's echo, whispers blend,
On paths of kindness, we will depend.
The warmth of hand in hand we find,
A refuge built, two hearts entwined.

A shelter soft against the storm,
In every hug, we feel the warm.
With gentle words, our spirits soar,
In this embrace, we ask for more.

Days will wander, seasons turn,
Yet through it all, our passions burn.
With open hearts, we share our care,
In every glance, a love laid bare.

So here we build, with strength and grace,
These bonds of care, a sacred space.
In trust, we rise, together fair,
A tapestry woven, rich and rare.

The Design of Gentle Touches

In softest strokes, the world awakes,
A tender touch, the heart remakes.
With whispers fine, our fingers trace,
Lines of connection, a warm embrace.

Each brush of skin, a silent song,
A melody where we belong.
In fleeting moments, life entwines,
Designs of love in gentle signs.

Warmth like sunlight, gentle and pure,
A craft of hearts, both strong and sure.
We build our world with every caress,
Creating beauty, a shared finesse.

From thumb to palm, our stories weave,
In every touch, we learn to believe.
A language soft, with feelings new,
In the art of caring, I find you.

So let us paint with tender hands,
A gallery where love expands.
In every touch, our spirits match,
The design of us, a perfect catch.

Embracing the Edges of Us

Along the borders, we collide,
In every fracture, love won't hide.
With open arms, we hold what's near,
Embracing edges, calm yet clear.

Our stories merge where shadows blend,
In carved-out spaces, we can mend.
With every glance, the world will see,
The beauty found in you and me.

In whispered dreams, we find our way,
Through tangled thoughts, bright hues display.
Together we dance, in full delight,
Embracing edges, love ignites.

Where differences mark our unique trace,
In the cradle of flaws, we find our place.
For in the cracks, our hearts are sewn,
Embracing edges, never alone.

So let us cherish, come what may,
The contours of us, night and day.
In unity's arms, above we rise,
Embracing edges, sharing skies.

Sculpted Sentiments

With every word, we chisel deep,
Sculpting feelings, truths we keep.
In marble dreams, our hearts compose,
Sentiments carved like a blooming rose.

Each gentle note, a crafted line,
In the gallery of love, you shine.
We mold our wishes with soft esteem,
Sculpted warmth, a tender dream.

In hands of care, our lives embrace,
Each pulse a stroke, a perfect grace.
With every breath, we craft new art,
Sculpted sentiments from the heart.

Through storms and calm, the shapes will form,
In every moment, love's soft warm.
With tools of trust, we shape the day,
Sculpted in joy, together stay.

So let us carve with passion's guide,
In sculptures true, we won't divide.
For in this art, our souls entwined,
Sculpted sentiments, love defined.

Staircases to the Soul

Step by step, we rise and fall,
Each turn reveals a hidden call.
Hand in hand, we trace the light,
In shadows deep, our dreams take flight.

Winding paths through fears and hopes,
Each staircase holds the love that copes.
With every step, we find our way,
Unlocking doors to a brighter day.

The whispers echo, soft and clear,
In silent moments, we draw near.
With every heartbeat, every sigh,
Our spirits dance, we learn to fly.

Between the landings, stories bloom,
In sacred spaces, we find room.
To breathe, to grow, to stand as one,
Together, face the rising sun.

At the top, we pause and stare,
Looking back on love laid bare.
These staircases lead us home,
In every heart, we need to roam.

Windows of Intimacy

Through glass we gaze, horizons wide,
Soft reflections of love inside.
Each glance a promise, soft and true,
In quiet moments, just me and you.

Open frames invite the light,
Gentle warmth in the darkest night.
We share our dreams, our fears, our tears,
In windows clear, love conquers fears.

Shadows dance, and laughter sings,
Each whisper shared, the joy it brings.
With every breath, we blend as one,
In this sweet space, our lives are spun.

Glass panes shield us from the storm,
In your embrace, I find my warm.
Our hearts entwined, a sacred space,
Within these walls, we find our place.

When night descends and stars appear,
We weave our dreams from visions clear.
Windows of intimacy vast and bright,
Together, painting worlds of light.

The Echo of Heartbeats

In every heartbeat, a story unfolds,
Rhythms of life, a treasure of gold.
Through silence between us, feelings grow,
An echo of love, in the undertow.

In crowded rooms, we find our tune,
A symphony played beneath the moon.
With every pulse, I feel you near,
In the dance of shadows, we conquer fear.

The world may fade, but we remain,
Two echoes entwined, in joy and pain.
Within this bond, time stands still,
An everlasting ink to fill.

Our heartbeats sync, a gentle refrain,
Binding us close, through joy and strain.
Each thump a whisper, a vow so deep,
In this sacred rhythm, love we keep.

When all is quiet, the noise subsides,
In the echo's embrace, love abides.
We share this pulse, so wild and free,
Together, just you and me.

Nestled in Togetherness

In quiet corners, we find our peace,
Wrapped in warmth, where worries cease.
Gentle whispers fill the air,
Nestled together, we lay bare.

The world outside may fade away,
In cozy nooks, we choose to play.
With laughter bright, and hearts aligned,
In this togetherness, love defined.

Fingers intertwined, steadfast and true,
In tender moments, I cherish you.
The glow of dawn wakes our embrace,
In every dawn, we find our grace.

With evening's hush, we claim the night,
Sharing dreams bathed in soft light.
The stars above bear witness still,
In our togetherness, hearts fulfill.

So here we sit, in this sacred space,
Time suspended, a warm embrace.
Nestled in love, we've found our way,
Together forever, come what may.

Shielded by Resilience

In storms that rage and winds that howl,
We stand our ground, resolve a cowl.
Through trials fierce, we hold the line,
With every challenge, we brightly shine.

Our spirits forged in fire and light,
We rise again, prepared to fight.
With hearts united, strong, and pure,
We'll face the darkness, we endure.

Together we stand, a mighty wall,
In shadows deep, we will not fall.
Our bonds unbroken, fierce and bold,
A tale of strength in every fold.

For every tear that's shed in pain,
A brighter day will surely gain.
We cultivate our garden bright,
In shared resilience, find our might.

With faith as our unyielding guide,
We carve our path, refuse to hide.
Through every challenge, trials vast,
Shielded by love, our fate is cast.

Nurtured by Kindness

In gentle whispers, we are sown,
A garden rich, where love has grown.
With every act, a seed we cast,
Nurtured by kindness, friendships last.

A smile exchanged, a helping hand,
In simple moments, we understand.
Compassion's touch, a soothing balm,
In chaos wild, we bring the calm.

Through darkened days and sunlit hours,
We gather strength like blooming flowers.
With kindness rooted deep and true,
Together we rise, in all we do.

In laughter shared, a bond is spun,
A tapestry of hearts as one.
With every heartbeat, every sigh,
Nurtured by kindness, we learn to fly.

So let us spread our wings of care,
In every kindness, love we share.
Together we weave a brighter tale,
Nurtured by kindness, we shall prevail.

The Fabric of Us

Threads of laughter, woven tight,
In every moment, day and night.
The fabric thick with memories spun,
Together as one, we have begun.

In colors bright, our stories blend,
Each woven tale, a cherished friend.
Through trials passed and joys embraced,
In every stitch, our love is laced.

The fabric strong, yet soft to touch,
Embroidered dreams and hopes as such.
With every challenge, we find our way,
In the fabric of us, we brightly stay.

And when the world feels torn and frayed,
Together we mend, our hearts displayed.
For in this quilt of shared delight,
We find our strength, we ignite the light.

In warmth and love, we thrive and grow,
The fabric of us, a steady flow.
With every heartbeat, this truth in praise,
Our bond, a treasure, through all our days.

Refuge in Each Other's Arms

When shadows dance and fears arise,
In each other's arms, the world defies.
A haven built with tender care,
A refuge found in love we share.

With whispered dreams and silent sighs,
Our hearts entwined beneath the skies.
In every storm that sweeps the land,
We find our strength, together we stand.

A shelter soft, where laughter flows,
In each embrace, the love just grows.
With open hearts, we face the night,
In refuge sweet, we find the light.

Through trials faced, we hold on tight,
In every shadow, we seek the light.
For in this bond, we're never alone,
Refuge in love, a comfort zone.

So let us cherish this sacred space,
In each other's arms, we find our grace.
With love as our guide, we'll never part,
In refuge shared, united heart.

Echoes of Endearment

Whispers linger in the night,
Soft and sweet, a gentle flight.
Memories we hold so dear,
Forever close, always near.

Laughter dances in the air,
Shared secrets, none can compare.
Moments etched in time and space,
A soft smile upon your face.

Through the storms and sunny days,
Unified in countless ways.
Our hearts sing a timeless song,
In this bond, we both belong.

Echoes of love softly call,
In every rise, and every fall.
Together, we walk hand in hand,
In the warmth of this love, we stand.

As twilight fades into the dawn,
In each heartbeat, love is drawn.
Endearments whispered, soft and low,
In our hearts, the echoes grow.

Carving Out Forever

With chisel sharp and steadfast hand,
We carve our dreams upon the sand.
Moments shaped by hopes and fears,
A sculpture born from sweat and tears.

Underneath the open sky,
Sculpted love will never die.
Each curve and line tells a tale,
Of love that blooms and will not pale.

Time may weather all we make,
Yet in our hearts, true bond won't shake.
For every crack tells a story,
Of battles won and fleeting glory.

Through trials faced and dreams pursued,
We carve our path, our souls imbued.
In every heartbeat, every sigh,
We build forever, you and I.

Our legacy etched with intent,
In every moment, love is spent.
As time goes on, and shadows fell,
We carve our tale, our stories tell.

The Frameworks We Build

With sturdy beams, we raise the walls,
A structure strong, that never falls.
Foundation laid with trust and care,
In this embrace, we're always there.

Each room a memory, bright and clear,
A tapestry of joy and cheer.
The windows frame the world outside,
In this haven, love resides.

Nails of laughter, screws of dreams,
Together, nothing is as it seems.
With every plank, our bond grows tight,
In every corner, love's pure light.

Through seasons change, we weather well,
In every storm, our spirits swell.
This framework holds our dreams alight,
In harmony, we share the light.

As years unfold, we build anew,
Each layer adding something true.
With every heartbeat, every thrill,
We shape our lives in love's goodwill.

Foundations of Friendship

In quiet moments, silence speaks,
A bond so strong, no words it seeks.
With laughter shared and tears we cry,
In every glance, we understand why.

Building trust, brick by brick,
In every joy and every trick.
Roots entwined in earth so deep,
A friendship grown, cherished to keep.

Through seasons change, we stand as one,
Under the shade of friendship's sun.
With every challenge that we face,
In this journey, we find our place.

Hand in hand, through thick and thin,
In every loss, we find our win.
The strength we share, a guiding hand,
In the love of friends, we understand.

As time goes on, and bonds evolve,
In laughter's light, our hearts revolve.
Foundations laid, we build anew,
Together, forever, just us two.

Mosaic of Mutual Understanding

In colors bright, we come together,
Each note a harmony, light as a feather.
With every piece, we start to see,
A world united, you and me.

Through varied shades, we learn and grow,
In whispered tales, our truths bestow.
The journey shared, a vibrant art,
Piecing together, heart by heart.

Where shadows linger, light will weave,
In mutual respect, we find reprieve.
With open minds, we bridge the gap,
A dance of thoughts upon life's map.

In every corner of our song,
Embracing differences, making us strong.
With gentle hands, we shape our fate,
A mosaic rich, no room for hate.

So hand in hand, let's build anew,
In this grand tapestry, me and you.
With every voice, a story flows,
Together in trust, our true self shows.

Emblems of Enduring Trust

In quiet spaces, bonds are formed,
With every promise, a heart warmed.
Through trials faced and laughter shared,
With steadfast faith, we're truly repaired.

A message sent, with no preset course,
Each open heart, a gentle force.
In loyalty's light, we pave the way,
Trust like a river, come what may.

In whispered secrets, strength will grow,
In every challenge, we face the flow.
Together we stand, with hands entwined,
An emblem strong, so well-defined.

Through storms we navigate, in grace we sail,
In trust, we flourish, we shall not fail.
Though time may test, our hearts endure,
In love's embrace, we find the cure.

So here's my vow, forever true,
In this shared journey, just me and you.
Together forever, as roots entwined,
An emblem of trust, beautifully designed.

The Silhouettes of What We Share

In every moment, shadows play,
Profiles merging, night and day.
In shared laughter, we intertwine,
A tapestry woven, yours and mine.

With gentle whispers, secrets flow,
Under starlit skies, our stories glow.
In etched outlines, we see the truth,
The silhouettes speak of our shared youth.

In quiet walks, where dreams align,
Imprints linger, yours and mine.
Each step we take, a dance defined,
In the fabric of time, our hearts combined.

As dawn awakens, colors bright,
Our silhouettes fade into the light.
Yet in the shadows, we'll always find,
The echoes of love that binds us kind.

With every heartbeat, a confirmation,
In this vast world, our shared foundation.
Together we flourish, together we care,
In life's grand canvas, we boldly share.

Foundations Balancing Dreams

On sturdy ground, we lay our plans,
In every vision, hope expands.
With dreams like seeds, we start to grow,
A foundation built, as our spirits flow.

In shared endeavors, our hearts align,
Strength in unity, a true design.
With every challenge, together we'll soar,
Balancing dreams, we reach for more.

In whispered wishes, futures gleam,
In every effort, we stitch the seam.
Foundations strong, we rise and climb,
In the dance of life, we beat in time.

Beneath the stars, we chart a way,
In every heartbeat, the promise sway.
Together we'll flourish, together we'll dare,
In the tapestry of dreams, we lay it bare.

So hand in hand, we forge our fate,
In every moment, we celebrate.
A foundation strong, a bond so true,
In the light of dreams, I stand with you.

Luminescence in Shared Spaces

In twilight hues, our laughter soars,
Soft whispers dance on wooden floors.
The warmth of words, an evening glow,
In shared spaces, love starts to grow.

Sunset paints the sky with grace,
Captured moments we can't replace.
Hands entwined, we breathe in sync,
In this cocoon, we never shrink.

Echoes of dreams in gentle sighs,
Glimmers of hope in caring eyes.
The world outside fades to a blur,
In our haven, nothing can stir.

Every glance, a quiet vow,
In the present, we choose now.
With shared light, we illuminate,
Each shadow that we navigate.

Together trapped in time's embrace,
Finding solace in this place.
Every heartbeat, a sacred song,
With you, I know where I belong.

The Edifice of Affection

Brick by brick, we build our home,
A sturdy shelter where we roam.
Each memory, laid with tender care,
A fortress strong against despair.

Windows wide to let dreams in,
The warmth of love is where we begin.
Within these walls, we learn to trust,
In every laugh, in every rust.

Foundations woven with gentle grace,
In solitude, we find our place.
Echoes linger, soft and sweet,
In this haven, our hearts meet.

Frames adorned with all our smiles,
Each room filled with endless miles.
From shared glances to tender fights,
This edifice ignites our nights.

As seasons change and time unfolds,
In the heart of this, our story holds.
Love, a structure we will share,
An edifice beyond compare.

Balconies of Vulnerability

High above, we share our fears,
In the silence, we wipe tears.
Open hearts in a fragile space,
Those balconies, our sacred place.

Skyline dreams with gentle sighs,
Two souls dance beneath the skies.
Fences high, but spirits free,
In our truth, we just can be.

Each confession, a fragile thread,
Woven tightly, compassion spread.
With every fall, we stand again,
On balconies, we learn to mend.

The dusk invites a secret glow,
A bond that only we can know.
Together we navigate the night,
In vulnerability, we find light.

With every breath, our spirits soar,
In gentle whispers, we explore.
Trust cascades like rain from skies,
On balconies where no one lies.

The Anatomy of Emotions

In chambers deep, our hearts reside,
A complex map we cannot hide.
Layers unfold, a tender song,
In this anatomy, we belong.

Muscles tense with fear's embrace,
Yet love can bring a gentle grace.
Veins of hope, pulse in our veins,
Through joy and sorrow, love remains.

Synapses sparking with dreams anew,
In every heartbeat, I find you.
Tissues woven with laughter's sound,
In this body, love is found.

Connective fibers, strong and true,
In the anatomy, it's me and you.
Every tear, each smile we trace,
Reveals the beauty of our space.

A balanced dance, our essence flows,
Through every ebb, our spirit grows.
Inside this body, together we roam,
The anatomy of our shared home.

Close Quarters of the Soul

In shadowed corners, we reside,
Whispers echo, hearts confide.
In silence, secrets often share,
The pulse of love hangs in the air.

Unraveled threads of life entwine,
In tangled thoughts, our spirits shine.
A dance of shadows, soft and bold,
Together, we are stories told.

With every glance, a spark ignites,
In close quarters, our love unites.
Through storms we weather, hand in hand,
Our souls a bridge, a sacred land.

In the quiet, trust is born,
Through laughter shared and hearts adorned.
A sanctuary, warm and bright,
In close quarters, we find our light.

And when the world feels far away,
In soul's embrace, we choose to stay.
Close quarters, a haven we create,
In this space, love resonates.

Loving Crafts of the Mind

Thoughts like colors blend and swirl,
In the canvas of our world.
With every stroke, imaginations fly,
Crafting dreams beneath the sky.

Weaving stories, old and new,
In loving crafts, our spirits brew.
Ideas blossom, take their flight,
In the garden of the mind, pure delight.

Each whisper formed through gentle hands,
Creating beauty, life expands.
In crafted moments, hearts unveil,
The art of love will never pale.

With every thought, a tender thread,
In shared creations, love is spread.
Through loving crafts, our souls align,
In the sanctuary, we intertwine.

As visions turn to vibrant light,
Our minds craft magic, day and night.
In every heartbeat, dreams defined,
In loving crafts, we are entwined.

Blueprints for Belonging

Drafting plans in heart's embrace,
Blueprints created for our space.
In lines that guide our journeys free,
A home where love can simply be.

Foundations laid in trust and care,
In every moment, memories share.
Together we design the way,
In blueprints drawn, we find our play.

With every laugh, a wall is built,
In sturdy bonds, no fear, no guilt.
The roof of dreams, both high and wide,
In blueprints forged, we take our stride.

The corners filled with warmth and light,
In every detail, hearts ignite.
A sanctuary for the soul,
In blueprints, we are truly whole.

From sketches rough to visions grand,
Together we will always stand.
In blueprints drawn, we find our song,
In belonging's arms, we all belong.

The Site of Shared Dreams

In twilight's glow, we gather near,
The site where dreams become sincere.
With open hearts, our hopes arise,
In whispered wishes 'neath the skies.

Each vision shared a spark ignites,
In bonded dreams, we find our flights.
The stars align, our pathways clear,
In the site of dreams, we have no fear.

Together woven, threads of fate,
In shared dreams, we captivate.
Hand in hand, we chase the night,
In this place, all feels so right.

As dawn approaches, colors blend,
In every dream, our spirits mend.
The site of shared dreams softly gleams,
In unity, we chase our dreams.

With every heartbeat, hopes endure,
In this site, our love is pure.
Together, we will always strive,
In shared dreams, we come alive.

Walls of Whispered Promises

In shadows cast by muted light,
Soft secrets linger, hearts take flight.
Each promise spoken, a silent thread,
We weave our dreams where words are said.

The walls hold echoes, long and deep,
Of laughter shared and wounds we keep.
In whispered vows, the shadows play,
As hope entwines the end of day.

Yet time can shake the strongest stone,
What once was ours feels overthrown.
But still we bend, not break, nor fall,
In whispered hopes, we rise, stand tall.

From these foundations, love does bloom,
In quiet corners, we find room.
For even walls, though cold and gray,
Can shelter warmth in their own way.

So let us build with gentle hands,
A fortress strong where kindness stands.
For in this space, our hearts align,
Within these walls, your hand in mine.

Intimacies in Stone

Beneath the arch of ancient arch,
Two souls collide in whispered march.
The coolness of the stone we tread,
Tells tales of love that never fled.

In the crevices of time and space,
We find the pause, we find the grace.
Each touch a spark, each glance a thread,
In this quiet world, our hearts are led.

The echoes of our laughter ring,
In the stillness, the stones can sing.
As we carve our names in timeless art,
Each groove a map of where we start.

With every step, the ground does know,
The stories shared, the seeds we sow.
Among the ruins of days gone by,
Intimacies in stone cannot die.

In shadows cast by dusk's embrace,
We find the warmth, we find our place.
For in the stone, our love's alive,
In every crevice, we deeply thrive.

Heartstrings and Frameworks

In the lattice of our days entwined,
Heartstrings pull, in rhythm, aligned.
Each frame a glimpse, a moment caught,
In every glance, a lesson taught.

They dance like shadows in our sight,
Creating art in the fading light.
With every stroke, we build anew,
A framework strong, a vibrant hue.

We thread our fears through silver lines,
With hopes that twine like creeping vines.
In tangled paths, we find our way,
Through heartstrings played, we learn to stay.

Each structure built in nights of care,
Forms a safe haven, shapes the air.
For in these forms, our dreams expand,
In heartstrings and frameworks, we understand.

As seasons shift, the colors change,
Yet love, it holds, through all that's strange.
With every breathe, our souls enmesh,
In heartstrings where new stories fresh.

The Geometry of Connection

Lines converge, a spark ignites,
In the space between, our hearts take flight.
Angles sharp, yet soft the touch,
In geometry of love, we find so much.

Circles spin, their paths entwined,
Every arc a treasure, beautifully defined.
Each point a memory, marked in time,
Where distance fades, and hearts align.

Triangles of trust, a sturdy base,
In this shape, we find our place.
The angles formed create a bond,
In the geometry of connection, we respond.

With every curve, we navigate,
Through the chaos, we create.
In patterns drawn beneath shared skies,
Our love's a blueprint, never dies.

So let us sketch in colors bright,
In the geometry, we'll take flight.
For through these shapes, our love will grow,
In every line, in every flow.

The Palette of Partnership

In colors bright, we blend our minds,
Each hue a thread, in life we find.
Together strokes, in laughter flow,
Creating visions only we know.

Your shade, my shade, together fine,
In every moment, our hearts entwine.
With every brush, our dreams ignite,
A masterpiece of pure delight.

Through trials faced, and joy embraced,
Our canvas grows, no space is wasted.
With trust our base, we paint the sky,
As partners strong, we'll always fly.

In every splash, a memory grows,
Echoes of us in vibrant shows.
The palette wide, our journey's call,
In shades of love, we stand so tall.

So let us share, this art divine,
With every stroke, our souls combine.
For in this life, with you I stand,
A palette bright, forever hand in hand.

Design of Dreams

In twilight's glow, our visions gleam,
We sketch our paths, a vibrant dream.
Each line a promise, strong and true,
A blueprint waits for me and you.

In whispered hopes, we draw the stars,
Designs adorned with love's sweet scars.
With every curve, our spirits soar,
A landscape vast, together more.

Through laughter's ink, our stories blend,
With every twist, our hearts transcend.
In colorful thoughts, horizons wide,
The dreams we share, our faithful guide.

Together we'll construct a fate,
With patience as we gestate.
In every plan, there's room to grow,
The design of dreams, ours to bestow.

So let us build, with every seam,
A world alive, with hope's bright beam.
For in this space, where passions stream,
We forge our lives, the design of dreams.

Silhouettes of Shared Stories

In shadows cast, our tales reside,
Silhouettes that in the dusk abide.
With every glance, a story told,
In whispered words, our hearts unfold.

In laughter's light, and sorrow's shade,
The moments shared shall never fade.
Each figure drawn, in light's embrace,
A tapestry of time and space.

Through tangled paths, we roam as one,
In dusk's warm glow, our fears undone.
With every step, our journeys blend,
Silhouettes of stories never end.

With memories stored in twilight's kiss,
We find connection, endless bliss.
As shadows dance, our spirits rise,
In silhouettes, our love defies.

So let us walk, through night and day,
With every dusk, we find our way.
Together bright, our stories soar,
In silhouettes, forevermore.

The Skeleton of Sentiment

Beneath the skin, our truths align,
A framework built, both yours and mine.
In quiet thoughts, our whispers dwell,
The skeleton of love we spell.

With every heartbeat, a pulse so strong,
In layers deep, we both belong.
The bones of trust, they intertwine,
In strength unseen, our hopes combine.

Through trials faced and lessons learned,\nIn every scar, our passion burned.
The structure firm, with grace we stand,
A skeleton of sentiment, hand in hand.

The marrow rich, vitality flows,
In memories shared, our garden grows.
With every laugh, and tear we share,
The skeleton of sentiment lays bare.

So let us build, on foundations true,
In love's embrace, just me and you.
For in this space, where hearts are lent,
We'll cherish what's, our sentiment.

The Nexus of Nostalgia

In corners of the faded room,
Whispers of laughter softly bloom.
Echoes of dreams, the tales reside,
Memories dance, never to hide.

Faded photographs, a window's glance,
Time unwinds in a wistful dance.
Lost moments linger, sweet and clear,
The heart remembers what it holds dear.

Fragments of time, like scattered leaves,
Each one a story, each one believes.
The warmth of the past wraps like a shawl,
In the nexus of nostalgia, we recall.

Footsteps echo on cobblestone streets,
Where childhood laughter and memory meets.
With each heartbeat, the past is near,
In the shadows, love casts its sphere.

Through the veil of time, we often roam,
In the dusk of dusk, we find our home.
In every sigh, and every smile,
Nostalgia bridges every mile.

Bridge of Understanding

Across the river, two worlds stand,
With hopes and dreams held in each hand.
Voices rise like a soothing song,
In the bridge of understanding, we belong.

Hearts open wide, with hands outstretched,
Empathy grows, no words seem etched.
In silence, we share the common pain,
Through the bridge, love flows like rain.

Differences fade, as light unveils,
In this realm where compassion prevails.
Together we stand, united, yet free,
In the bridge of understanding, you and me.

Every story shared, a vital thread,
Weaving our lives, where fears are shed.
In every heartbeat, a rhythm found,
On this bridge, connection resounds.

With open minds, we learn to see,
In shades of color, you and me.
A tapestry woven with care,
On the bridge, love's roots lay bare.

The Architecture of Unity

In the blueprint of our shared dreams,
Lies the strength of collective themes.
Brick by brick, our stories intertwine,
In the architecture of unity, we shine.

With every voice, a foundation laid,
In harmony's embrace, we aren't afraid.
Walls of trust, ceilings of grace,
In every corner, hope finds its place.

Through whispers of kindness, we build the way,
Together, we thrive, come what may.
The beams of love create our home,
In the architecture of unity, we roam.

A mosaic of cultures, colors, and dreams,
In its beauty, the future gleams.
With every heartbeat, every sigh,
In this unity, we learn to fly.

Challenges rise, but we stand tall,
In togetherness, we conquer all.
A sanctuary for every heart,
In the architecture of unity, we start.

Heartstrings Intertwined

Two souls dance in the evening glow,
With whispers soft, like the falling snow.
In every glance, a story spun,
Heartstrings intertwined, we become one.

Side by side, in laughter and tears,
We craft a bond that time reveres.
Every heartbeat whispers your name,
In this harmony, love's wild flame.

Moments shared, like waves on sand,
In the ebb and flow, we firmly stand.
With every storm, together we strive,
In the magic of love, we come alive.

Through every trial, we find our way,
In the tapestry of night and day.
With hands entwined, we dream and soar,
In heartstrings intertwined, we want more.

From dawn to dusk, through life we glide,
In every heartbeat, love's gentle tide.
In a world of chaos, we'll always find,
In every echo, heartstrings entwined.

Solidarity in Every Brick

In every brick, we lay our strength,
Bound together at arm's length.
With every wall that we create,
We build a bond that will not break.

Through trials faced, we hold our ground,
In unity, our hearts are found.
Each structure tells a story true,
Of hands that labored, me and you.

Through storms that rage and winds that wail,
We stand as one, we will not fail.
For every crack, a patch we make,
In solidarity, we awake.

Let love be poured into each seam,
Together, we pursue the dream.
In every brick, a pledge we find,
We lift each other, hand in kind.

So here we stand, both firm and wide,
In every heart, we will abide.
For solidarity we choose,
In every brick, we shall not lose.

The Landscape of Tenderness

Amidst the hills, a soft embrace,
Where kindness blooms in every place.
With gentle hands, we sow the seeds,
Of love that meets the heart's deep needs.

In twilight's glow, shadows will play,
Each moment cherished, come what may.
Through whispered words and silent grace,
We carve a world that we can trace.

The rivers flow with empathy,
Reflecting all that we can be.
In every tear, a tale we weave,
Of moments when we choose to believe.

Together we traverse the land,
With open hearts, we take a stand.
In every step, we leave a mark,
A testament in light and dark.

As dawn breaks forth and dreams ignite,
We hold each other through the night.
The landscape blooms, resilience bright,
In tenderness, we find our light.

Cornerstones of Trust

With every word, a bridge we build,
Our spirits strong, our hearts fulfilled.
The cornerstones of trust we lay,
In bricks of honesty each day.

Through laughter shared and sorrows known,
In every moment, love has grown.
With open arms, we face the storm,
Together, we create the norm.

In silence held, we find our peace,
As ties of trust will never cease.
Through trials faced and dreams pursued,
In unity, our hearts renewed.

For every promise made with care,
Our bond will flourish in the air.
With every step along the way,
We craft a trust that will not sway.

So here we stand, our hands entwined,
With cornerstones of love defined.
In every heartbeat shared with you,
Trust builds a path, steadfast and true.

Vaulted Ceilings of Joy

Beneath the arches, laughter rings,
In vaulted ceilings where joy springs.
Each moment shared, a glimmering light,
In every day that feels so bright.

Through every trial that we embrace,
We find the strength in every space.
With every smile that sparks the air,
Joy dances lightly everywhere.

In fleeting time, we capture bliss,
In whispered dreams, a tender kiss.
Through all the storms, we find our grace,
In every heart, a sacred place.

Together we create a song,
With notes of hope that make us strong.
The vaulted ceilings hold our dreams,
In joyful chords, our spirit gleams.

As twilight fades and stars appear,
We gather close, dispelling fear.
In every heart, joy finds a way,
In vaulted ceilings, we shall stay.

Strong Veins of Kinship

In shadows cast by family trees,
Roots dig deep, beneath the breeze.
Together we rise, through thick and thin,
A bond forged strong, where love does begin.

Laughter echoes in every room,
Hearts entwined, dispelling gloom.
Through trials faced, we stand as one,
Connected always, 'til the day is done.

Through whispered secrets and shared dreams,
Belief in each other, or so it seems.
A tapestry woven with threads of gold,
In every story, our truth unfolds.

Old photographs, memories fade,
Yet the love remains, never to jade.
In every heartbeat, our history flows,
Strong veins of kinship, forever it grows.

Together we walk, hand in hand,
Navigating life, together we stand.
In the circle of family, strong and bright,
Our hearts beat in harmony, day and night.

Connecting Spaces of Warmth

In a cozy nook, by the fire's glow,
Words like blankets, soothing, slow.
Within these walls, comfort we find,
A sanctuary built for hearts entwined.

Echoes of kindness fill each thread,
Where warmth resides, no heart can dread.
Gathering close, in laughter we share,
Connecting spaces, love fills the air.

Moments treasured, the small and grand,
A gentle touch, a helping hand.
In shared silence, the bond does grow,
Through whispered sighs, our spirits flow.

Every meal shared, every glance,
A dance of souls, 'neath fate's sweet chance.
Together we weave a tapestry bright,
In these spaces, our hearts take flight.

When the storms of life loom dark and wide,
In each other's warmth, we find our guide.
Through every trial, our love will stay,
Connecting spaces, come what may.

The Echoing Hallways of Love

In shadows deep, where memories tread,
The hallways echo, where soft words spread.
Each step we take, a story to tell,
Of laughter shared, or farewells that fell.

Sunlight dances on faded walls,
Remnants of joy that silently calls.
In rooms adorned with forget-me-nots,
Love's gentle whispers, time cannot blot.

With every corner, a moment held tight,
A touch, a kiss, in soft moonlight.
The pathway winds through days long gone,
Yet in our hearts, the warmth lingers on.

In the quiet corners, hope does bloom,
Filling the spaces, chasing the gloom.
The echoing hallways, a passage so dear,
Carry the tales of those we hold near.

Through every adventure, and timing's grace,
These halls surround us, a sacred space.
In love's embrace, we find our way,
Echoing softly, come what may.

Murmurs in the Walls

In the creaky joints and whispering beams,
Resides the echo of old-fashioned dreams.
Murmurs of laughter, heartstrings entwined,
Stories etched in the wood, dear and kind.

While the shadows drape in soft retreat,
Every murmur holds tales bittersweet.
Secrets shared beneath starlit skies,
In the stillness, love softly sighs.

Gentle reminders in corners so small,
Of years gone by, and the rise, the fall.
In those soft whispers, the past comes alive,
In the walls, our memories thrive.

Time may pass, but these echoes will stay,
In the fabric of life, they weave a way.
Through murmurs and sighs, a symphony calls,
Resounding love, in the heart of these walls.

With each shadow cast, history calls,
In the stories woven, our legacy sprawls.
As long as we're here, their song will resound,
Murmurs in the walls, forever profound.

Endeavors of Emotion

In shadows deep, where whispers dwell,
Hearts weave their tales, a silent spell.
Every heartbeat holds a dream,
In the ebb and flow, emotions gleam.

With every tear, a story flows,
In laughter's arms, sweet warmth grows.
Through trials faced and moments shared,
The depths of love, we have declared.

In simple touch, a spark ignites,
Binding our souls on starry nights.
Through valleys low, and peaks so high,
Together we soar, like birds in the sky.

With every glance, a promise made,
In gardens lush, our fears do fade.
Endeavors brave, with passions bright,
We chase the dawn, embracing light.

In quietude, our bond takes flight,
An endless dance, both day and night.
Through smiles and sighs, we find our way,
In the tapestry of love, we stay.

The Garden of Growing Love

In the dawn's embrace, flowers bloom,
Petals whisper soft, dispelling gloom.
Through seasons' change, we nurture and care,
In the garden of love, a bond we share.

Roots intertwine beneath the earth,
From tiny seeds, we find our worth.
With every drop of rain that falls,
Our love it grows, as nature calls.

Sunshine kisses leaves that sway,
In tender light, we find our way.
With laughter sweet, the blooms arise,
Radiating hope beneath clear skies.

In moments low, we plant anew,
Tend our hearts, with a gentle hue.
Through wild storms and gentle days,
Our garden thrives in countless ways.

As twilight falls, stars come to play,
In our secret space, love finds its way.
A eternal bond, with roots so deep,
In the garden of love, our hearts will keep.

Translucent Passages of Care

Through translucent paths, we walk so slow,
With gentle whispers, love starts to grow.
In every glance, a story is spun,
In the tapestry woven, two hearts become one.

Holding hands in the light of day,
Navigating shadows, we find our way.
With every heartbeat, we craft a song,
In the melody of care, where we both belong.

In quiet moments, with eyes that speak,
Together we rise, together we seek.
Through trials faced, and dreams we dare,
Every step taken, a passage of care.

As seasons shift and time moves on,
In the warmth of love, we have grown strong.
Through translucent layers, our truths reveal,
In a world so vast, it's warmth we feel.

In every hug, a universe shared,
In delicate moments, we've always cared.
Through translucent passages, side by side,
In the essence of love, our hearts abide.

Close Foundations of Joy

In laughter's echo, we find our peace,
Close foundations of joy, never cease.
With every smile, we build our home,
In the embrace of love, we're never alone.

Through trials faced, and lessons learned,
In the fires of life, our passion burned.
With hands held high, we'll face the storm,
In close foundations, we keep each other warm.

In all the little things we do,
The spark of joy keeps shining through.
With gentle words and heartfelt care,
In life's tapestry, our love we share.

Our hearts, a rhythm, in perfect time,
In this dance of life, so sublime.
Through every glance, our spirits soar,
In this haven of joy, we crave for more.

As seasons change, and moments flow,
In the garden of joy, we nurture and grow.
With love as our anchor, we stand so tall,
In close foundations of joy, we have it all.

Labyrinth of Longing

In shadows deep, my heart does roam,
Seeking whispers of a distant home.
Each twist and turn, a silent plea,
In this maze of hope, I long to be free.

The walls they close, yet dreams expand,
Mapping out where my soul will land.
A flicker of light through the veils of night,
Guiding me softly, a beacon so bright.

Paths intertwined, I wander slow,
Yearning for truth, where wildflowers grow.
But every step, a choice I find,
In the labyrinth's heart, I'm confined.

Memories echo, they dance and fade,
Crooning songs of the love we made.
Each corner turned, a bittersweet kiss,
In this intricate dance, I'm lost in bliss.

Yet through the twists, hope shall prevail,
With each heartbeat, I'll chart the trail.
Emerging from shadows, arms open wide,
In this labyrinth of longing, forever I'll bide.

Curves of Companionship

In laughter and tears, our stories entwine,
Winding paths that are yours and mine.
With every curve, our bond does grow,
In the dance of life, together we flow.

Through valleys deep and mountains high,
Shoulder to shoulder, we reach for the sky.
In silence and words, our spirits blend,
In the warmth of connection, we find a friend.

The curves may twist, but trust remains,
In the heart's embrace, joy breaks the chains.
With every heartbeat, a promise we make,
To cherish each moment, for love's sweet sake.

Through storms we weather, hand in hand,
In the tapestry of life, we take our stand.
Every curve, a picture framed,
In the gallery of us, love is named.

So here's to the bends, the turns we take,
In the landscape of friendship, we leave a wake.
Embracing the journey, come what may,
In the curves of companionship, forever we'll stay.

Mosaic of Moments

In fragments scattered, life's colors blend,
Each moment a jewel, around the bend.
A mosaic of laughter, heartache, and glee,
Telling stories of who we're meant to be.

Glimmers of joy, like sunlight's caress,
Shimmer through trials, crafting our dress.
With every heartbeat, a piece finds its place,
In this beautiful chaos, we trace the grace.

Memories linger, like paint on a wall,
Urging us forward, whenever we fall.
In the patchwork of time, our symphony plays,
Marking the chapters of all our days.

The edges may fray, but the picture is whole,
Each piece tells a tale, nourishing the soul.
In every heartbeat, in all that we see,
The mosaic of moments, our legacy.

So cherish each shard, the bright and the dark,
For in their embrace, we leave our mark.
Together we craft, with love as our guide,
In this mosaic of moments, we take pride.

Beams of Support

In twilight's glow, we stand in line,
With beams of support, our hearts align.
Through mountains and valleys, together we rise,
With hands intertwined, we touch the skies.

In silence and laughter, the bond that we share,
Carries us gently through life's wild glare.
With whispers of courage and shouts of delight,
Each beam a promise, illuminating the night.

In storms we may falter, but never we fear,
For in unity's strength, we hold each other near.
Through trials we weather, our spirits ignite,
In the warmth of together, we find our light.

With anchors of friendship, we weather the tide,
In the safe embrace, we no longer hide.
Each beam of support, a strength we impart,
Binding us close, heart to heart.

So here's to the bonds that lift us up high,
In the glow of connection, together we fly.
With beams of support, in the tapestry spun,
We navigate life, two souls become one.

Ramps of Kindness

In shadows cast by doubt, we stand,
With open hearts, we lend a hand.
Each gentle touch, a bridge we build,
In kindness' name, our spirits filled.

A smile shared, a moment bright,
Eases burdens, brings delight.
Through every act, a ripple flows,
In unity, our compassion grows.

The road is long, yet we won't tire,
Our brightening souls, a burning fire.
Together we rise, together we shine,
On ramps of kindness, hearts entwine.

Each step we take, each word we say,
Washes the darkness, lights the way.
With every deed, the world we mend,
In kindness' arms, we find a friend.

So let us weave a vibrant thread,
With every kindness that we spread.
In this tapestry of love and grace,
Ramps of kindness, our shared embrace.

Embraced in Timelines

In the fabric of time, our stories entwine,
Each moment a thread, each heartbeat a sign.
Through laughter and tears, we navigate space,
Embraced in timelines, we find our place.

Whispers of history dance in the air,
Echoes of memories, moments we share.
Past and present, they weave a strong bond,
In the tapestry of time, we gladly respond.

Futures await, with dreams bright and bold,
In the arms of tomorrow, our tales will unfold.
With hope as our compass, we dare to explore,
Embraced in timelines, we seek evermore.

In the footprints we've left, in the paths yet to roam,
We gather our courage, we build our home.
In the heart of the journey, no step is in vain,
Embraced in timelines, through joy and through pain.

Together we rise, as one, hand in hand,
With time as our witness, our dreams take a stand.
The stories we tell, in harmony's song,
Embraced in timelines, where we all belong.

The Heart's Blueprint

In every heartbeat, a story resides,
A map of our dreams, where love abides.
Lines drawn with purpose, in passion's embrace,
The heart's blueprint leads us to grace.

Through valleys of sorrow, through mountains of hope,
We navigate life, learning to cope.
With courage entwined in each choice that we make,
The heart's blueprint guides us through every quake.

In laughter and tears, we sketch our design,
With colors of joy, where the sun starts to shine.
Each curve a reminder of love's gentle touch,
The heart's blueprint whispers, "You're never too much."

As friendships are born, and passions ignite,
The heart's blueprint glimmers in soft, steady light.
Together we build, with dreams intertwined,
In the heart's grand design, true beauty we find.

So cherish the maps that our hearts create,
In the story of love, we find our fate.
With every connection, our legacies grow,
The heart's blueprint sings, guiding us to glow.

Tiers of Togetherness

In layers of life, we find our way,
Built from connections, come what may.
Each tier a promise, a bond to embrace,
In tiers of togetherness, we carve our space.

With every step, we lift one another,
In joys and in sorrows, we find a brother.
Through struggles we climb, hand in hand we rise,
In tiers of togetherness, love never dies.

The laughter we share, the dreams that we weave,
Strengthens our hearts, in what we believe.
From the roots to the branches, our spirits extend,
In the tiers of togetherness, we find our blend.

As seasons do change, our bond stays the same,
In the dance of our lives, we play the same game.
With each layer built, our fortress stands tall,
In tiers of togetherness, we conquer it all.

So cherish the moments, the love we have sown,
In the fabric of time, we've together grown.
With hearts intertwined, we sing a sweet song,
In tiers of togetherness, we always belong.

The Geometry of Us

In angles sharp, we meet each glance,
Two lines that draw in perfect dance.
A circle's curve, a gentle touch,
In every shape, we feel so much.

With pi and rays, our paths align,
Through x and y, a love divine.
The symmetry in every space,
A measured pause, a warm embrace.

In fractals deep, our hearts entwined,
A design unique, a thread unlined.
Each vertex holds a whispered vow,
In every point, we wonder how.

From edges raw to softened scenes,
We craft our story in the seams.
In shadows cast, our light remains,
In every curve, love's sweet refrains.

Archways of Devotion

Beneath the arches, love does frame,
A quiet vow, a whispered name.
The stones stand firm, the wood caressed,
In sacred halls, our hearts are blessed.

With every step, the echoes call,
Through light and dark, we will not fall.
In every curve, in every rise,
A promise held 'neath open skies.

The ivy grows on walls so strong,
Each leaf a note to love's sweet song.
Embraced by nature, hand in hand,
In timeless grace, we take our stand.

In arches wide, our laughter rings,
A chorus born from simple things.
The shelter found in love's embrace,
In every breath, a sacred space.

Blueprint of Belonging

Lines sketched out, our dreams unfold,
On paper bright, our stories told.
In every draft, our hopes ignite,
With every sketch, we find the light.

The plans we make both soft and bold,
In silent whispers, hearts console.
The roofs we build, the walls we raise,
A haven made in sunlit rays.

With colors bright, we paint the past,
In strokes of joy that seem to last.
Each room a space where laughter flows,
In every corner, love proudly grows.

A foundation strong, our roots go deep,
In bonds we forge, the promises keep.
The blueprint drawn, no line erased,
In every heartbeat, we are embraced.

The Art of Togetherness

In strokes of kindness, we connect,
In colors shared, hearts intersect.
With brushes held, our dreams collide,
In canvas wide, we laugh and ride.

Each layer painted, shade and hue,
In every moment, me and you.
The palette rich, a blend of souls,
Together strong, we become whole.

With every splash, a tale unfolds,
In vibrant strokes, our love beholds.
The masterpiece of days well spent,
In joyful whispers, our hearts bent.

In twilight's glow and dawn's embrace,
In every frame, we find our place.
The art of us, a symphony,
In harmony, just you and me.

Milton Keynes UK
Ingram Content Group UK Ltd.
UKHW021954151124
451186UK00007B/250